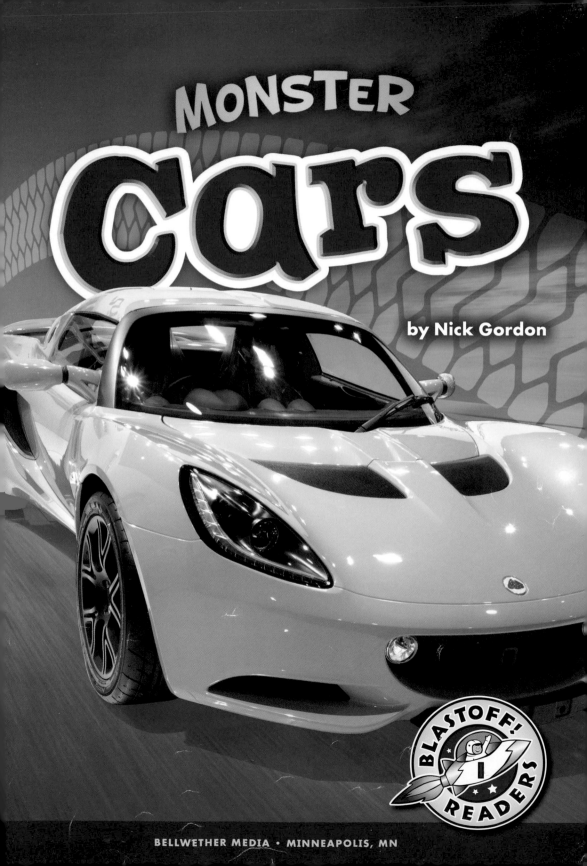

# MONSTER Cars

by Nick Gordon

BELLWETHER MEDIA · MINNEAPOLIS, MN

Note to Librarians, Teachers, and Parents:

**Blastoff! Readers** are carefully developed by literacy experts and combine standards-based content with developmentally appropriate text.

**Level 1** provides the most support through repetition of high-frequency words, light text, predictable sentence patterns, and strong visual support.

**Level 2** offers early readers a bit more challenge through varied simple sentences, increased text load, and less repetition of high-frequency words.

**Level 3** advances early-fluent readers toward fluency through increased text and concept load, less reliance on visuals, longer sentences, and more literary language.

**Level 4** builds reading stamina by providing more text per page, increased use of punctuation, greater variation in sentence patterns, and increasingly challenging vocabulary.

**Level 5** encourages children to move from "learning to read" to "reading to learn" by providing even more text, varied writing styles, and less familiar topics.

Whichever book is right for your reader, Blastoff! Readers are the perfect books to build confidence and encourage a love of reading that will last a lifetime!

This edition first published in 2014 by Bellwether Media, Inc.

No part of this publication may be reproduced in whole or in part without written permission of the publisher. For information regarding permission, write to Bellwether Media, Inc., Attention: Permissions Department, 5357 Penn Avenue South, Minneapolis, MN 55419.

Library of Congress Cataloging-in-Publication Data

Gordon, Nick.
 Monster cars / by Nick Gordon.
 pages cm. – (Blastoff! readers: Monster machines)
 Summary: "Developed by literacy experts for students in kindergarten through grade three, this book introduces extreme cars to young readers through leveled text and related photos"–Provided by publisher.
 Audience: K-3
 Includes bibliographical references and index.
 ISBN 978-1-60014-935-1 (hardcover : alkaline paper)
 1. Automobiles, Racing–Juvenile literature. I. Title.
 TL236.G654 2014
 629.222–dc23
                                          2013006852

Printed in the United States of America, North Mankato, MN.

# Table of Contents

Monster Cars!      4

Special Parts      8

Super Engines      16

Glossary      22

To Learn More      23

Index      24

# Monster Cars!

Super fast cars
roar down
the road.

Race cars speed along **drag strips**. They also go around racetracks.

## Special Parts

Cars need special parts to go really fast.

A **spoiler** is on the back of many fast cars. This slices through the air.

spoiler

Many race car tires are wide and smooth. They help the race cars make fast turns.

Sometimes race cars use **parachutes** to slow down!

**parachutes**

# Super Engines

Fast cars need powerful **engines**. The engines are loud.

The fastest car on
the road has a
**turbo engine**.

Race car engines have a lot of **horsepower**. They help the cars fight for first!

# Glossary

**drag strips**—long, straight tracks used for races between two cars

**engines**—the parts of vehicles that produce power

**horsepower**—a measure of the power an engine produces

**parachutes**—large pieces of cloth that fill with air to slow something down

**spoiler**—a wing-shaped part on the back of a car; it helps the car slice through the air.

**turbo engine**—a type of engine that burns fuel faster to create extra power

# To Learn More

## AT THE LIBRARY

Alpert, Barbara. *Fast Cars*. North Mankato, Minn.: Capstone Press, 2013.

Clark, Willow. *Cars on the Move*. New York, N.Y.: PowerKids Press, 2010.

Pipe, Jim. *Fantastically Fast Cars*. Mankato, Minn.: Smart Apple Media, 2012.

## ON THE WEB

Learning more about fast cars is as easy as 1, 2, 3.

1. Go to www.factsurfer.com.

2. Enter "fast cars" into the search box.

3. Click the "Surf" button and you will see a list of related Web sites.

With factsurfer.com, finding more information is just a click away.

# Index

air, 10

drag strips, 6

engines, 16, 18, 20

fast, 4, 8, 10, 12, 16, 18

horsepower, 20

loud, 16

parachutes, 14, 15

parts, 8

race cars, 6, 12, 14, 20

racetracks, 6

road, 4, 18

slices, 10

slow, 14

smooth, 12

speed, 6

spoiler, 10, 11

tires, 12

turbo engine, 18

turns, 12

wide, 12

The images in this book are reproduced through the courtesy of: Citybrabus, front cover; Ron Kimball/ Kimball Stock, pp. 4-5; KKulikov, pp. 6-7, 8-9; Cjmac, pp. 10-11; Natursports, pp. 12-13; Mirafoto/ Glow Images, p. 13 (small); Action Sports Photography, pp. 14-15; Michael Stokes, pp. 16-17; Max Earey, pp. 18-19; Luis Louro, pp. 20-21.